Ketut, Boy Wood Carver of Bali

by JUDITH M. SPIEGELMAN

Photographs by Mallica Vajrathon and Henky Pantoc

Eleven-year-old Ketut, the Fourth-Born, knows that his island of Bali, one of the 3,000 islands that make up Indonesia, is famed for the excellence of its artists. Ketut's own village of Mas is a wood carving village, and his two brothers are carvers. Ketut, too, wants to carve. He spends all his free time carving, but usually he has to work very hard.

He must pound rice with his mother to earn money, since his father is too old and his brothers are at the master carver's shop all day. He must remember to get clean well water and make offerings to the gods at the family's temple. Because there are few textbooks in Bali's schools, he spends hours copying his lessons off the blackboard.

Nevertheless, Ketut is overjoyed when the master carver sees his work and accepts him into the shop. At first Ketut is only allowed to do sanding or polishing, and to make copies—all beginner's tasks. But Ketut learns quickly and soon has an expensive piece of wood on which to work. Like all carvers, he studies the wood's grain until the carving is clear in his mind's eye before beginning.

After long months of hard work, Ketut offers his work to the master carver during *Tumpak Wayang*, the festival honoring the arts. What happens next, not only surprises Ketut, but makes him and his family very proud.

Text and photographs combine to reveal the warm appeal and rich splendor of this unique island culture and people.

Jacket by Marjorie Zaum K.

Ketut,
Boy Wood Carver
of
Bali

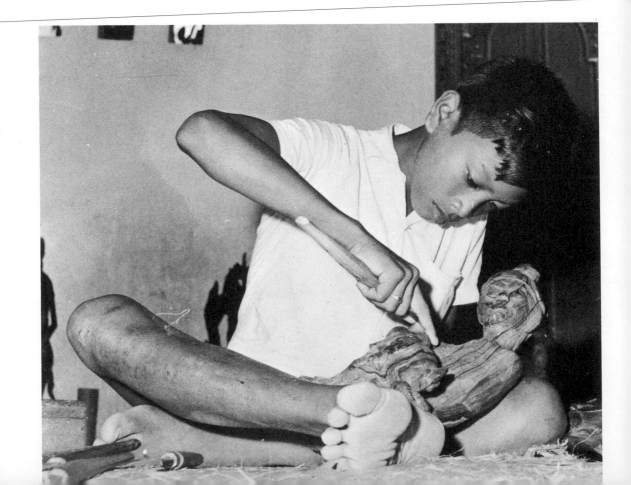

Ketut,
Boy Wood Carver
of
Bali

by JUDITH M. SPIEGELMAN

Photographs by Mallica Vajrathon
and Henky Pantoc

Julian Messner New York

Picture Credits

Mallica Vajrathon: 9, 13, 14-15, 17, 19, 21, 27, 30, 33, 36, 37, 38, 39, 40, 41, 43, 44-45, 46, 47, 48, 54, 56, 58, 61, 63

Henky Pantoc: 12, 16, 18, 23, 24, 25, 28, 50, 51, 60, 62

Indonesian Tourist Board: 11, 53

Published by Julian Messner, a division of Simon & Schuster, Inc.
1 West 39 Street, New York, N.Y. 10018. All rights reserved.

Copyright, © 1971 by United Nations Children's Fund (UNICEF).

Printed in the United States of America
ISBN 0-671-32415-2 Cloth Trade
     0-671-32416-0 MCE
Library of Congress Catalog Card No. 71-146484
Design by Marjorie Zaum K.

For my good friend, Dr. A. A. Djelantik,
a prince of Bali, now Medical Officer
with the World Health Organization in Iraq.

AUTHOR'S NOTE

In developing this book around the life of Ketut Gampil, boy wood carver of Mas, I was fortunate in having the help of Dr. Hildred Geertz, of the Anthropology Department of Princeton University. The understanding of and insight into Bali's unique culture which she provided were invaluable.

I am also grateful to Miss Anak Agung Gde Muter of the Indonesian Mission to the United Nations for her assistance, and to the officers of the Asia Society who helped on four books in this series—including this one.

In Bali itself, among the many people who helped make my brief stay productive and pleasant were Karseno Sosmojo, formerly with the UNICEF office in Djakarta; Tjokorde Mas of Ubud; and Ida Bagus Tilem, who provided the warmest of Balinese hospitality. As a frequent visitor to Ketut's house, I still remember the cries of alarm with which Ruru's six-month-old baby greeted my daily arrival. Somehow the wailing infant helped bring me closer to Ketut and his family, and I hope the gods will continue to bless their lives and their work.

J.M.S.
October, 1970

UNICEF

UNITED NATIONS CHILDREN'S FUND · FONDS DES NATIONS UNIES POUR L'ENFANCE

UNITED NATIONS, NEW YORK

Dear Boys and Girls,

In their needs and in their dreams, children everywhere are very much the same.

The clothes they wear, foods they eat, games and holidays they enjoy may be far different from our own. But there isn't a boy or girl anywhere in the world who doesn't need exactly the same things you do to grow up healthy and happy: love and care; food, shelter and clothing; a chance to play and a chance to learn.

Above all, children share the same hopes of becoming mothers and fathers, nurses, doctors and teachers, heroes and helpers when they grow up.

The purpose of this book, as well as the others in this series, is to help you understand what life is like for real children growing up today in various parts of our world. And if you can go beyond understanding them, if you can try and imagine yourself in their place, it may be a very important thing. It could truly help to bring peace in our world that much closer.

For as the great poet from Chile, Gabriella Mistral said, "When the children of the world understand each other, then we shall indeed have peace on earth."

Paul B. Edwards
Director of Information
UNICEF

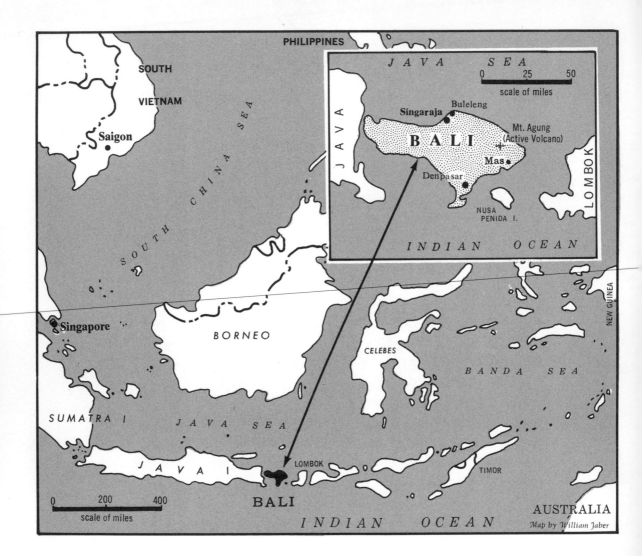

PHILIPPINES

SOUTH

VIETNAM

Saigon

SOUTH CHINA SEA

Singapore

BORNEO

CELEBES

SUMATRA I

JAVA SEA

JAVA I

LOMBOK

BALI

BANDA SEA

TIMOR

NEW GUINEA

AUSTRALIA

INDIAN OCEAN

0   200   400
scale of miles

Map by William Jaber

JAVA SEA

0   25   50
scale of miles

JAVA

Singaraja   Buleleng

BALI

Mt. Agung
(Active Volcano)

Mas

Denpasar

NUSA
PENIDA I.

LOMBOK

INDIAN OCEAN

At first, no one paid any attention to the carvings that Ketut, the Fourth-Born, made. After all, he lived on Bali, an Indonesian island famous for its artists, and he lived in Mas, a village famous for its wood carving. In Mas, boys carved wood the way children in other "craftsmen" villages of Bali learned to paint, carve stone, or work in gold and silver.

Ketut's oldest brother, Ruru, the First-Born, was a grown man with children of his own. He was an expert carver, and he taught Ketut how to choose wood free from worms and how to handle a carving knife. Soon, Ketut spent all his free

time by whittling little animals and birds from the pieces of wood he found about the village.

One day, Ketut carved a strange little bird hopping on one leg. Ruru noticed it right away and took it to the nobleman for whom both he and their brother, Lantur, the Second-Born, worked.

Nobleman Tilem, whose title, Ida Bagus, means "Eminent and Beautiful" was the son of a great carver, and was a master carver himself. He held the little bird in his strong hands and said to Ruru: "Imagine an eleven-year-old boy carving like this! I see the spirit of the artist has made it come alive. Tell your young brother he can have a place in our workshop, but that it takes a long time to become a carver. He must begin the years of training now. Yes, one day there may be still another carver in your family."

That night, Ruru told Ketut what Ida Bagus Tilem had said. Happiness lit up Ketut's face. Who would have believed that the gods would bring this about? If anyone could judge carving, Ida Bagus Tilem could. And he was saving a place for Ketut in his workshop, an honor that would be given to only a very few of the boys in Mas.

Ketut's *memé* (Balinese for mother) was far from happy at the news. Although she was proud of her youngest child, she grumbled: "The boy's arms are needed at home to help. I am not a young woman anymore. And your father is too sick to work. Who will help me pound rice while the boy learns carving? As it is, he can only help me in the afternoon after school. And just look how many mouths we have to feed!" She pointed to her five grandchildren.

It would have been easy to feed the many mouths, if only Ketut's family had owned rice lands, as their neighbors did. The farmers in Bali, as well as in the other islands of Indonesia, grow two—and sometimes three—crops of rice under

the year-round tropical sun. Without rice land, Ketut's family had to earn a living by carving wood and by pounding rice for rich farmers—when they could get work.

Bapa (father) was old, and his arms were too weak to raise the heavy wooden pestle high and drop it down in the mortar again and again. Ketut's two older brothers were busy almost all day at the workshop. As for his older sister, the Third-Born, she was married and lived with her husband. So Memé depended on Ketut to help her every day, for it took strong arms to free the rice grains from their husks.

"I'll help just as before, Memé," Ketut promised. "If only I can learn to be a carver, I'll pound rice as fast as other people beat the *kulkul* when there's a fire!"

Memé had to smile. The kulkul was the high, carved bell tower that stood at the village crossroads. When there was a fire in the village, neighbors beat a fast *rat-a-tat-tat-tat* on its great gong, as an alarm signal.

"It is possible," Ruru said, "that the boys in Ida Bagus Tilem's workshop get paid pocket money if they learn quickly. With the help of the gods, our Ketut may bring home money for rice, Memé, sooner than you think."

So it was decided that Ketut would continue helping Memé, but that beginning the following day, he would also go to the nobleman's carving school.

The next morning, Ketut was up before the sun. The air was still chilly. The sarong he slept in was damp from the dew which had seeped into the half-open sleeping hut he shared with his brother Ruru's children. The whole family lived together in a house compound, a group of small huts surrounded by a wall.

Ketut slipped past the separate huts where each of his married brothers and their wives slept. At the well, he washed his body quickly, and dressed in his school clothes: a clean white shirt and short pants. Then, crumbling a small piece of rice stalk in his hands, he rubbed it across his teeth to clean them. Ketut was now ready to start this important day in his life.

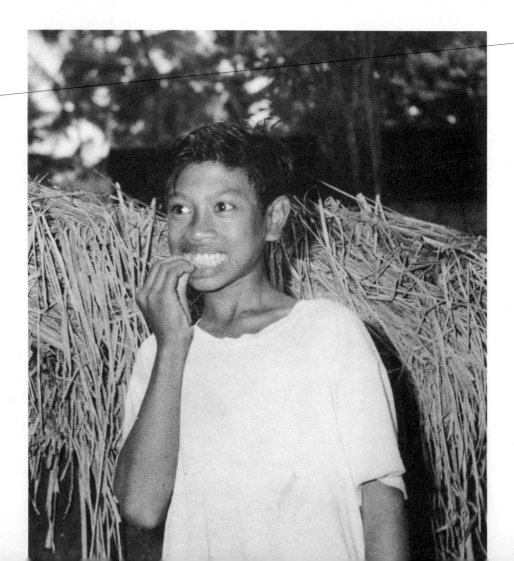

He brought a pailful of clean well water to the kitchen hut. Memé was ready to boil two large pots of rice. Rice was their main food, and every morning she boiled enough to feed the family for the whole day.

"The hot coals," she reminded Ketut. Taking an empty coconut shell, he went to the sweet-seller's stand, which was just a few doors from their house. From the fire which kept her coffeepot hot, the shopkeeper filled Ketut's shell with burning coals. All the while, Ketut kept looking at the delicious toffees and sugarcane she sold, but today he had no *rupiahs* to buy any.

"Titiang nunas, titiang nunas," he said, thanking her twice in Balinese, and hurried home. Memé threw the coals into the clay stove, and soon the dried grass and twigs caught fire. The water in the huge black metal rice pot began to boil. From time to time, Memé blew into the fire through a bamboo tube, to keep it alive.

As soon as the rice was boiled, Memé prepared a tray with many small squares of banana leaf on it. On each leaf, she put some rice, salt, a dash of chilipepper, and a fresh flower. No one ate breakfast until offerings had been made to the Hindu gods the Balinese believe in, for Bali is the one island of Indonesia whose people are still Hindu. On most of the other islands, people follow the Moslem religion.

Ketut usually made offerings at their house temple for the entire family. Every day they worshipped at a group of small god-houses, or shrines, set up on high stone columns

in one corner of their courtyard. The shrines faced toward Mount Agung which means "great mountain" in Balinese. Mount Agung, which the Balinese believe to be the home of the gods, is the highest mountain in all of Bali, and the holiest. Ketut knew that it is also an active volcano. In 1963, it had erupted, killing more than a thousand people. By some miracle, those people who were inside the temple which was located halfway up the mountain's slopes were spared.

Ketut set offerings before the shrine of each of the three great Hindu gods: Brahma, Lord of Fire; Vishnu, Lord of the Waters; and Iswara, Lord of the Earth. He also placed an offering for the souls of his forefathers, whom the Balinese also believe to be gods. Holding a freshly picked flower between his fingers the way Memé had shown him, Ketut waved his hand several times in the direction of the mountain, inviting the gods again and again to come down and accept the offerings.

Every day, Ketut asked the gods to bless each member of his family. Today, he also asked them to make his arms strong for rice-pounding and his hands sure for carving. As he moved from shrine to shrine, his white dog, Dapur, followed at his heels, hoping Ketut would drop some rice. Ketut also made offerings to the demons or evil spirits which the Balinese believe are everywhere.

20

Having shared their food with the gods and evil spirits, everyone served himself from the big rice pot. Ketut had just begun eating when the school bell rang. "It must be almost seven o'clock," Ketut thought. It was time for classes to begin. He gulped down the rest of his rice.

"Hurry—the school bell—where are your notebooks?"

Memé prodded him. More than anything else, she and her husband wanted their youngest child to learn to read and write, something they had never been able to do. They knew that when Ketut could read and write like the priests, teachers, and nobles, he would be respected in their village.

Ketut ran to the sleeping hut and scooped up his notebooks and pencils from under his rope bed. Memé gave him five rupiahs, less than two pennies, for his midmorning snack, and he scurried out of the compound.

As he rushed past, Ruru called out, "Remember, Fourth-Born, come to the carving workshop today after the rice is pounded. Ida Bagus Tilem wants you to come." As if Ketut could forget!

Leaving his house, he hurried out into the wide, dirt street. As he walked on, the streets became crowded with

women carrying great loads of coconuts, bananas, mangoes, vegetables, flowers—all grown in Bali—on their heads. The women were on their way to market, which was held at the crossroads every third day.

As usual, the streets rang with the sounds of hammers and chisels from the carving workshops. But this morning, it was like music to Ketut's ears. Soon, he might be working in a carving workshop himself—if only Ida Bagus Tilem didn't change his mind.

But there was no time to think about that now. He had arrived at school. It was an airy building, with no walls or doors. The thick thatched roof protected the children from the burning sun and, during the rainy months, from the drenching rains which are common in Southeast Asia.

The other boys and girls had already taken their seats. Ketut found his seat, a hard wooden bench he shared with another boy.

"Slamet pagi, Bapak Guru" ("Good Morning, Father Teacher"), the children greeted their teacher, Regreg. They seldom called Regreg by name. Instead, they used the most honored title Bapak Guru, or "Father Teacher." A lady teacher was called Ibu Guru, or "Mother Teacher."

"Slamet pagi," the teacher answered in Indonesian from his place in front of the fifth-grade class. Indonesian has been the language used in government schools ever since 1945, when Indonesia became free of Dutch rule. At home, the children spoke Balinese, which they learned as a second language at school.

Ketut watched as some of the different children took small bundles of uncooked rice to Bapak Guru. There are not enough teachers in Indonesia, and this is how the parents show their gratitude to them for helping their children. Most of the teachers have to teach two—sometimes three—different grades. The United Nations Children's Fund is helping the government train more teachers. Still, the government cannot afford to pay the teachers much money. So parents send them the most precious gift of all—rice. When his family could spare it, Ketut also brought rice to school.

From his badly worn arithmetic textbook, Bapak Guru began to write the first lesson of the day on the blackboard. Ketut took out his notebook and copied the lesson. Every day, the children copied the lessons and recited them together, for the teacher had the only set of books in the fifth grade.

Textbooks are needed everywhere in Indonesia. It would

take millions of them to meet the needs of every student in the country. Ketut's class needed books for history, geography, science, arithmetic, and Indonesian—the subjects they

learned in the fifth grade. In Bali, children also learn about the Hindu religion, while the children on the other islands study the Moslem religion in school.

When recess came at nine o'clock in the morning, the children streamed out into the bright sunlight. Most of them, including Ketut, headed for the nearest snack stand. He bought some hot, spicy gruel which was served on a banana-leaf plate, for which he paid five rupiahs. Squatting down beside the stand, Ketut scooped up the soft gruel slowly, using a little spoon of banana leaf. He enjoyed this spicy mixture of garlic and onions, which was sprinkled with grated coconut.

The sun felt hot, so Ketut headed for the shadiest spot of all, beneath the enormous branches of a banyan tree. His best friend, I Made, was there, pitching coins with another boy. Ketut could only watch, for he had spent his pocket money on the gruel.

Soon the recess ended, and the boys and girls went back to school. At eleven o'clock, the school day was over. Today, Ketut didn't dawdle with his friends, but hurried home instead. There was only one thought in his mind. How many baskets of rice were waiting to be pounded? If he finished early enough, he could go to the carving workshop. As he got closer to their house compound, Ketut heard Memé pounding. As he crossed the courtyard, the ground beneath his feet shook from her thumpings.

There were two baskets of rice to be pounded. Memé told him they belonged to Tjokorde Mas, one of the wealthiest men in the village. He would pay her in rice as usual, but it might take them all afternoon to finish. Without a word, Ketut picked up the heavy wooden pestle that lay on the ground and began to pound.

There is a rhythm to rice-pounding. When two people pound together, each has to work with the same rhythm.

Ketut knew it well. It was like the beat that Lantur, the Second-Born, used when he played the small gongs in the village orchestra—fast, steady, strong. Together, Ketut and Memé pounded for hours, never missing a beat.

The day was getting hotter and hotter. The sun was directly overhead. "It must be at least one o'clock," Ketut thought. Memé stopped to rest. Even though his arms and shoulders were aching, Ketut kept on pounding. He had to use both hands now, and his rhythm was getting slower. Memé took her club up once more, and together they pounded the rest of the rice.

"We have finished, Fourth-Born," she said. "I will sift the rice clean and carry the bushels to Tjokorde's compound myself. There is still time now for you to clean your hands and face and present yourself at the workshop. But remember to speak to Ida Bagus Tilem in high Balinese, or else he may become angry and not invite you to sit among the carvers."

Memé's words made Ketut happy. After all, she too wanted him to become a carver! As for high Balinese—the special language spoken only to nobles, priests, and the gods —he hoped the right words would come to him.

With his shirt tucked neatly inside his sarong, and his hands and face washed clean, Ketut walked to the noble-man's compound as fast as he could. But he did not go in right away. He stood there for a long time, staring at the high, split, stone gate. A richly carved stone demon guarded each side. It was only fitting that Ida Bagus Tilem should have such a gate, for he was one of the leading artists in Mas, as his father, grandfather, and great-grandfather before him had been.

Ketut was afraid. Would he ever be as good as either of his brothers? Suppose he were given a precious piece of wood to carve and a demon caused it to split in two under his chisel? Suppose the right words for addressing a noble in high Balinese stuck in his teeth?

Somehow, Ketut shook off his fears, and finally, he walked past the fang-toothed demons guarding the gate. Inside, he saw a lovely, wide courtyard. There were many pavilions with handsome carved doors, thick flowering shrubs and trees, and a shop with high glass windows. The shop faced the main road, and only the best carvings made in the workshop were displayed on the shelves and tables. Some of Ruru's carvings, and a few done by Lantur, had been chosen for display in the shop.

Following the sound of many hammers tapping, Ketut soon found the long porch where some twenty carvers and five young boys sat cross-legged on a floor mat, at work. This was Ida Bagus Tilem's carving workshop and school.

Ketut was relieved to see Ruru and Lantur. Each of them was bent over his carving, holding it firmly between his feet, making the chips fly as his knife cut into the wood.

Ruru looked up first and saw Ketut. "Ida Bagus Tilem isn't here just now, Fourth-Born. He must be in the shop. Just wait. He'll come back soon."

Ketut stood to one side, trying not to show how nervous

33

he was. He wondered what would happen when the nobleman came back.

Finally, the slim, young noble appeared. He was no older than Ruru. His curly black hair framed his face, and like any other villager, he was dressed in shirt and sarong. On his fingers, two gold rings gleamed.

In a low voice, Ruru presented Ketut. "Ida Bagus Tilem, here is my youngest brother."

Ketut stood there, quiet and shy. As Memé had taught him, he bent his head down so it would not be higher than the noble's. He also cast his eyes down, for it wasn't polite to look directly into the eyes of such a highly respected person. Ketut's mouth was dry and his heart began to pound as he waited for Ida Bagus Tilem to speak.

"So," the nobleman thought, "this is the boy who carved the strange little bird! A tall boy—this one must be around twelve. He had been just that age when his father, the master carver, Ida Bagus Njana, began teaching him to use a carving knife. How shaky he had felt that day, and how long ago it all seemed now!"

"You may work here," he told Ketut. "You may sit down there and be your brother's helper." To Ruru, he added: "A beginner must begin at the beginning. Let him start with the sanding and polishing."

34

Ruru made room alongside him on the straw mat for his brother, and Ketut took his place among the carvers.

Ruru started by giving Ketut a statue he had made, which still had knife marks on it. He showed his brother how to sand the marks smooth by rubbing a gritty pumice stone over the carving and how to polish it with a piece of bamboo.

By the end of the afternoon, Ketut had rubbed the statue until it was wonderfully smooth to touch. He had buffed it until the teak wood was a rich, gleaming brown. Now, it was ready to stand in the window of the carving shop, where visitors came, expecting to see—and to buy— some of the best carvings in all of Bali.

At four o'clock, the carvers packed up their tools and put their rough carvings in one corner of the porch. The young apprentices stopped too. Ruru motioned to Ketut to sweep up the wood shavings and chips and carry them to the nobleman's kitchen. The youngest and newest boy always did this chore.

When he had finished, Ketut stopped to admire the strange and wonderful carvings which decorated the courtyard. There were many richly carved palace doors, painted gold, which had once belonged to kings of Bali. And, hanging on a tree, he saw a clown's face carved on a coconut

shell. It was such a funny face that Ketut grinned right back at it. How good it felt to relax, now that his first afternoon as a carving apprentice was finally over.

Ketut's grin soon vanished when he caught sight of a beautifully carved Garuda bird. The sacred bird was perched high on a pedestal. It seemed charged with magic. Surely the gods had guided the hands of whoever had carved it. Ketut wondered if he would ever be able to carve anything as good. Or would he always be just the youngest brother of Ruru and Lantur? Would Ida Bagus Tilem ever think of him as Ketut the carver? Ketut made up his mind to work hard and prove he was good in his own right.

Soon, he reached the *balé bandjar*, the meeting hall, and he decided to go in. Inside, the men were at their favorite pastime, playing with their fighting cocks. Ruru was among them, getting his favorite white cock ready for a practice fight against a red one. To excite his bird, he swung it up and down in the air and ruffled its neck feathers. It was a good practice fight, and the two owners agreed that their birds would fight at the next important temple festival.

The cock fights in the village were exciting. The men cheered and shouted and called out their bets. Boys could not take part, but they were allowed to watch. The winners usually took home purses full of rupiahs. Not long ago, the

wealthy farmer, Tjokorde Mas, had been among the winners. He had given his winnings to the town council, to pay for repairing the roof of Ketut's school.

Ruru let Ketut hold his bird and stroke its downy back. Ketut was sad to see it go back into the cage, but he was allowed to carry the cage home.

Once there, Ketut and his four-year-old niece, Varsi, went to the community bathing place to shower before supper. Ketut knew it was too late to sing and play as the children usually did in the showers. Any moment darkness might fall, for it comes suddenly in Bali.

And darkness was the time when demons roamed. Twilight was just as dangerous. Ketut and Varsi washed and dried quickly, then hurried to the safety of their house compound.

A dinner of rice and spiced baked eels was on the stove, and whoever was hungry took down a china plate and served himself. While it was still light, Ketut and Varsi ate. Later, they helped Memé wash the dishes and put them away.

By then a deep, velvety darkness had fallen. Ketut had no homework that night, so there was no need to light the kerosene lamp. Because kerosene cost so much, they used the lamp as little as possible. Ketut wished he had gone to his best friend's house while it was still light. He wanted to tell I Made about being allowed to work in Ida Bagus Tilem's workshop. But it was better not to walk alone after dark unless one had to.

The kulkul rang five times. This was the signal for the musicians who belonged to the *gamelan* (orchestra) to meet. Like many Balinese, Ketut's brother Lantur was as talented in music as in art. He had been chosen to play the small gongs in the orchestra. Most of the other members were rice farmers by day and musicians at night.

Lantur and Ketut walked over to the meeting hall where the musicians rehearsed every night. Ketut felt safe, for the evil spirits didn't usually harm people who walked in two's or three's. At the crossroads, Ketut saw the carved demons on the kulkul tower. The demons, which were meant to frighten away evil spirits, stood out clearly in the bright moonlight.

The meeting hall was full of people who had come to watch the orchestra and dancers practice. Mothers sat around the edges of the hall, holding infants in their arms, while the older children hoped for a chance to play. People in each neighborhood wanted their gamelan to be the best in the village.

Each player sat on the floor, with his instrument beside him. Ketut sat behind Lantur and the twelve-gonged instrument he and three other men played. From time to time, Ketut got a chance to hit the gongs with the padded sticks and send out deep rippling sounds. Lantur pressed Ketut's hand so that he knew just when to strike them. The boy was thrilled to play the gongs, and he and three other players worked together as if they were one man.

Then, a young girl Ketut knew from school came to the middle of the floor. At the drummer's cue, she began swaying and twisting in time with the music. Her teacher

watched every move. The girl was practicing the dance she
would offer to the gods at the big temple festival which was
to be held soon. Now, she practiced in her white school

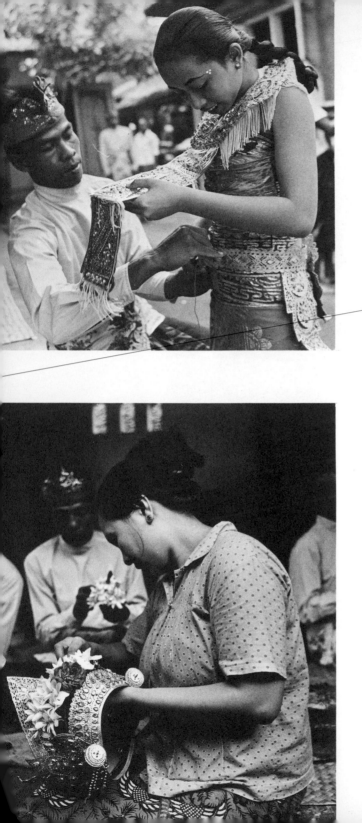

blouse and short dark skirt. But at the temple, she would wear make-up, a beautiful costume with a sash of gilt cloth, and a great helmet of gold trimmed with fresh frangipani flowers. Girls, some as young as five years old, were chosen to begin learning the dances for which Bali is famous all over the world.

About ten o'clock, the rehearsal ended, and everyone went home. But Ketut could not fall asleep that night. He kept thinking about his first day at the workshop and that he had passed only his first test. If he could learn fast enough and keep pleasing Ida Bagus Tilem, he had the chance to become a master carver one day. But many more tests lay ahead of him. Praying that the gods would continue to guide and protect him, Ketut finally fell asleep.

The next afternoon after school, Ketut again took his place among the carvers. This time, Ruru set a small carving of a fat-bellied man on the floor beside Ketut. The statue was so small it fit in Ketut's hand. "Copy this carving," Ruru told his younger brother, and he gave Ketut a piece of light-brown fruitwood called *sawo*. Sawo is a good wood for beginners because it is soft and therefore easy to carve. Since there are many of these fruit trees in Bali, the wood is cheap, so it didn't matter if the apprentices spoiled their carvings.

During the rainy months which followed, Ketut made copy after copy of the fat-bellied man. This was the way all beginners learned. He ruined some of the pieces, but in time, he began turning out almost perfect copies.

One day, Ida Bagus Tilem showed Ketut a large wooden bell, carved in the shape of a head. The bell hung from a tree in the courtyard. It was the work of Tilem's father, the master carver. Ketut knew that Ida Bagus Tilem must be pleased with his work, or else he would not have asked an apprentice to make a copy of his father's work.

But this task wasn't as easy as it looked. At first, Ketut

got the ears too big and the nose lopsided. Then, Ida Bagus Tilem sat down beside him and showed him how to scale the ears down and make the nose even. Ketut sanded and

polished, and when the little bell was finished, he placed it in front of the master carving on the tree. Anyone comparing the two could see that the small one was a good copy, but Ketut knew he was far from being a master carver. Still, just being able to make a copy of a master carving made him feel good inside.

But Ketut's biggest test was yet to come. One day, he would have to work with one of the costly hard woods imported from the Indonesian islands of Java or Borneo—shiny black ebony, or reddish-brown teak, or spicy-smelling sandalwood. Then he would have to carve something original—from an idea of his own—the way Ruru and the other good carvers did. Ketut was eager to try, but he was not sure how such a carving would turn out.

That evening, Ketut forgot all about carving, as his friend, I Made, brought the news that a shadow play was to be presented in the village. This is a special kind of puppet show usually held by the light of a coconut-oil lamp. The flat puppets usually represented heroes, heroines, gods and goddesses, giants, demons, huge birds, snakes or elephants, or even clowns. Children and grown-ups listened to the *dalang* (puppeteer) act out all the parts. The gamelan accompanied him with music. This was Ketut's favorite kind of entertainment.

The shadow play began around ten o'clock in the evening, and it was not over until dawn. But Memé and the other mothers never worried. If there was a shadow play anywhere in the village, they knew their children would be watching the shadow figures move across the white-cloth screen for the whole night.

Ketut joined the other children outside the house of the family who had ordered the shadow play in honor of their daughter's wedding. The dalang had already stretched his white-cloth screen between two bamboo poles, and people were seated on the ground before it.

That night, the dalang acted out one of the great Hindu legends, the capture of Queen Sinta by the King of Demons and the battle to free her. Ketut and his friends had seen this shadow play many times before. Yet for hours they watched every move.

Queen Sinta (left) and King of Demons (right)

The play began as the Demon King carried the sobbing Queen Sinta off to a faraway island.

Most thrilling of all was the rescue scene, in which Hanuman, King of the White Monkeys, leaped across the ocean to find Queen Sinta. Then, leading his monkey army, he battled the demon army, which was led by a fierce giant. Hundreds of arrows whistled across the screen, and both monkeys and demons groaned as they fell to their death.

The battle noises were so exciting that Ketut forgot that the characters were only shadows. It seemed to him they were real gods, goddesses, and giants. He stayed until dawn, waiting until the Queen was finally freed and returned safely home to her king. Good had won out against evil. Now, Ketut could go home happy.

At the compound, everyone was just getting up. The weary Ketut had just enough time to make the daily offerings, eat some rice, and stumble to school.

That morning, Bapak Guru stood near the blackboard. Instead of writing the day's lessons on the board, he said: "I have some wonderful news this morning. The wooden cases in front of you have just come by ship from Djakarta. You know that is our nation's capital. From now on, there will be no more copying lessons from the blackboard!"

The children looked at each other in amazement.

55

"As soon as we can get these cases open, I will give each of you a set of four books. You will guard them well, and tomorrow you will bring in covers to keep them clean. You will learn everything inside these books, from cover to cover. Our government printed these books. The paper came from far across the seas—from the United Nations Children's Fund—enough to print almost twelve million textbooks. I expect that, from now on, each of you will learn twice as much, twice as fast. Now who will help me open these cases?"

As sleepy as he was, Ketut offered to help. Soon, all the cases had been opened, and the books had been given out to the excited children. Ketut counted his set of books; there were four in all: one each for history, arithmetic, and

science, and an Indonesian reader, with many stories and pictures. Carefully, he touched the pages of each book. Now that there would be no more copying, the work would go so much quicker. It seemed almost too good to be true.

During recess, the children spoke about their books, and about what they would find to use as covers for them. Ketut wondered if Memé would give him an old sarong. Until they had covers for them, Bapak Guru told the children to put the books back in the wooden cases.

Before school had ended for the day, Ketut was wishing he had not gone to the shadow play. He yawned and stretched, and he wanted to put his head down and sleep. "Suppose there is a lot of rice to pound!" he thought. "How will I ever do it?" But this was his lucky day. There had been only one basket to pound, and Memé had finished it by herself.

When Ketut got to the carving workshop, it seemed that his lucky day had really come. At long last, Ida Bagus Tilem gave him a large piece of valuable teak wood. "It is time for you to start a carving of your own," he said. "Look long at the wood, until some shape in it calls out to you. But always remember, you must have the carving 'in your belly' before you pick up your knife."

Ketut knew just what the nobleman meant. None of

the carvers worked from sketches. But they saw clearly in their minds what they wanted to carve, and they could feel the carving down to their fingertips. The first thing Ketut did was to hold the wood in his hand to feel its weight. He turned it this way and that, staring at the swirls of grain in the wood until they almost danced. All afternoon he stared at the wood, but no shape called out to him.

Finally, by the end of the afternoon, he saw a figure in the wood. A grin of relief broke over his face. In the wood, he saw Ruru, squatting on his heels and holding his white cock close to his body. Ketut closed his eyes. He

clearly saw Ruru hugging the bird to his side. The figure was still there when Ketut opened his eyes. He knew he was ready to start his first real carving.

For days and weeks, Ketut showed no one what he was doing. Day after day, he sat in a corner, away from the other carvers. He wanted this carving to be all his own work. He didn't want anyone to help him. Secretly, Ketut watched Ruru whenever he held his pet white bird. This helped Ketut keep the carving "in his belly." At night, he prayed that the gods would help guide his hands. Days, he kept on working in spite of a blister on his hand.

Soon it was Tumpak Wayang, the festival honoring the arts. Puppets, masks, and dance costumes were set out in the sun. Ida Bagus Tilem, his carvers, and the apprentices cleaned and polished their carving tools. During this festival, artists honored the tools they used by giving them special care.

That night, people brought special offerings to the many temples in the village. Dressed in his best sarong,

Ketut carried an offering of flowers, bananas, oranges, and cones of rice on his head. The women and girls who glided down the road to the temple also carried offerings—some two feet high—on their heads. Not a single offering fell. Hundreds of offerings were piled on the temple altars, and many were things of beauty. The priest prayed that the gods would not let the fine arts of Bali die out. Then he moved among the people, sprinkling a few drops of holy water on each one. Ketut also drank some of the holy water, and he

washed his face in it three times. This gave him the gods'
protection and blessing.

After he had been sprinkled with holy water, Ketut felt
he was ready to finish his carving. He sanded and polished
it, and then he put it down in the middle of the carving
porch so that Ida Bagus Tilem would see it.

Some time later, the nobleman came by. When he saw
the carving, he stared at it for a long time. He ran his hands
over its smoothness. He turned it all the way around, and
then back again. He kneeled down beside it to take a closer
look. Then he spoke: "I think this carving belongs in our
shop. It is a real carving—yes—this is a fine carving. There is

another carver in your family, another wood carver in Bali."

Ketut was so proud and happy that he wanted to jump about the yard. Instead, he picked up a new block of wood, and began to study its rippling grain.

As he worked over his new carving, Ketut remembered the day he had first stood outside this courtyard. That afternoon, the gods surely must have given him the courage to walk through the high, split, stone gate. They had guided his hands in making a carving good enough to be displayed. He would make special offerings to them tomorrow.

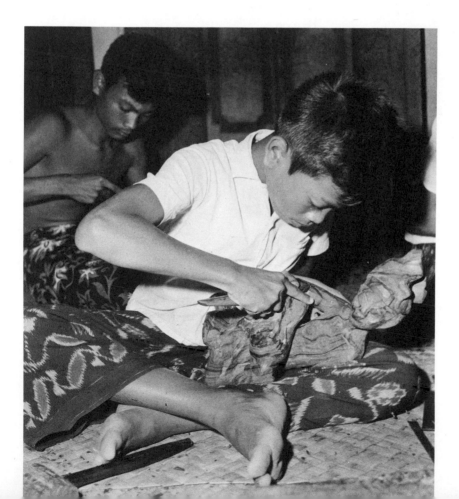

HOW TO PRONOUNCE FOREIGN WORDS
(The syllable in capital letters is to be accented.)

Agung	AH-goong
alang-alang	uh-LANG uh-LANG
balé bandjar	BAH-lay BAHND-jahr
Bali	BAH-lee
Banyan	BAHN-yahn
Bapa	BAH-puh
Bapak Guru	BAH-pah GOO-roo
Brahma	BRACH-mah
dalang	DAH-lang
Dapur	dah-POOR
Djakarta	djah-KAR-tah
gamelan	GAH-mah-lahn
Garuda	gah-ROO-dah
Hanuman	hah-NEW-men
Ibu	IH-boo
Ida Bagus Tilem	EE-dah BAH-goose TIH-lehm
I Made	ee MAH-day
Indonesia	in-doe-NEES-yah
Iswara	ess-WAH-rah
Ketut	keh-TOOT
kulkul	KOOL-KOOL
Lantur	lahn-TOOR
Mas	MAHS
Memé	meh-MAY
Njana	NYAH-nah
Regreg	rehg-REHG
Ruru	roo-ROO
rupiahs	roo-pea-YAS
sawo	sah-WOE
Sinta	SIN-tah
Slamet pagi	SLA-met pah-GEE (hard "g" as in "girl")
Titiang nunas	tet-YAHNG noo-NAHS
Tjokorde	djoh-KOR-dah
Tumpak Wayang	toom-PAHCK why-YAHNG
Varsi	VAR-see
Vishnu	VEESH-noo

64